Contents

Some words are printed in bold, **like this**. You can find out what they mean by looking in the glossary.

What is divorce?

When a man and a woman get married, they usually **intend** to stay married forever. However, sometimes it doesn't work out that way. Many couples divorce, and many children and teenagers become part of these divorced families.

Divorce is when two people end their marriage. It is a **legal** arrangement and must be finalized, or made official, in court.

Not so rare

In the past, divorce was unusual and shocking. There was a lot of social pressure on families to stay together, and divorced people could be outcasts. Things have changed quite a bit since that time. Today, divorced families are very common. Many people come from divorced families, and if they don't, they probably have a relative or friend who does.

Divorce can be a very difficult time for a family.

Joanne Mattern

Heinemann

www.heinemannlibrary.co.uk

Visit our website to find out more information about Heinemann Library books.

To order:
☎ Phone 44 (0) 1865 888066
🖹 Send a fax to 44 (0) 1865 314091
💻 Visit the Raintree bookshop at www.heinemannlibrary.co.uk to browse our catalogue and order online.

Heinemann Library is an imprint of Capstone Global Library Limited, a company incorporated in England and Wales having its registered office at 7 Pilgrim Street, London, EC4V 6LB – Registered company number: 6695582

Heinemann is a registered trademark of Pearson Education Limited, under licence to Capstone Global Library Limited

Text © Capstone Global Library Limited 2009
First published in hardback in 2009
Paperback edition first published in 2010

Edited by Kristen Truhlar, Rachel Howells, and Louise Galpine
Designed by Richard Parker and Manhattan Design
Picture research by Mica Brancic
Production: Victoria Fitzgerald

Originated by Chroma Graphics (Overseas) Pte Ltd
Printed and bound in China by Leo Paper Products Ltd

British Library Cataloguing in Publication Data
Mattern, Joanne, 1963-
Divorce. - (The real deal)
155.9'3

A full catalogue record for this book is available from the British Library.

Acknowledgements
We would like to thank the following for permission to reproduce photographs: © Alamy pp. **10** (Photofusion Picture Library), **18** (Adrian Sherratt), **20** (Travelshots.com), **24** (AceStock); © Bubbles pp. **14, 25**; © Corbis pp. **6** (Jon Feingersh/A1 pix), **9** (Bilderlounge), **12** (Michael Prince); © Getty Images pp. **11** (Benelux Press), **16** (Stone), **13**; © Jupiter Images p. **7** (BananaStock); © Masterfile p. **26** (Michael A. Keller); © Rex Features p. **15** (David Pearson); © Photolibrary pp. **21** (Bubbles), **27** (Image100); © SuperStock pp. **4** (Image Source), **5** (Brand X), **8** (Pixland), **19** (Jiang Jin), **22, 23** (BananaStock), **17**.

Cover photograph of a torn wedding photograph reproduced with permission of © iStockphoto (S. K. O'Donnell); cover photograph of a wedding ring reproduced with permission of © iStockphoto (bluestocking).

We would like to thank Anne E. Pezalla for her invaluable help in the preparation of this book.

Every effort has been made to contact copyright holders of any material reproduced in this book. Any omissions will be rectified in subsequent printings if notice is given to the publishers.

Disclaimer
All the Internet addresses (URLs) given in this book were valid at the time of going to press. However, due to the dynamic nature of the Internet, some addresses may have changed, or sites may have changed or ceased to exist since publication. While the author and publishers regret any inconvenience this may cause readers, no responsibility for any such changes can be accepted by either the author or the publishers. It is recommended that adults supervise children on the Internet.

Divorce and separation

Divorce is different from **separation**. Sometimes a husband and wife will decide to live separately for a while. During this time, they usually try to work out the problems in their marriage. Separation does not end a marriage. If the couple cannot work out their differences, they may then go on to get a divorce.

Divorce is difficult for everyone involved. The couple are usually sad and angry that their marriage did not work out. Their children are scared about what the future will hold. They have many questions and wonder what it will be like to live in a family that is not together. Divorce can bring many changes. It is normal to have changing feelings about divorce.

Getting a divorce is a big decision, and most couples give it a lot of thought.

NEWSFLASH

For many years, statistics claimed that half of all marriages ended in divorce. Recent studies have shown that more than 40 percent of all marriages end in divorce. Marriages that have lasted for a number of years are less likely to end in divorce than marriages that are only a few years old.

Why do parents divorce?

Parents may divorce for many reasons. A husband and wife may change over the years. They may become interested in different things and find they have little in common. They may not enjoy spending time together anymore.

Parents can also drift apart if they spend too little time together. Sometimes one or both parents become so involved in work or a hobby that they stop spending time with the family. Parents may discover they no longer have things in common after a while.

Changing opinions

A husband and wife may not share the same opinions about important issues. These differences in opinions may lead them to argue a lot and lose respect for each other. In time, some couples decide they would be happier if they went their separate ways.

Case study

Jamie's parents were always arguing, yelling, and slamming doors. It all seemed pretty normal to Jamie. Then one day, his mum and dad sat down with Jamie and told him they were getting a divorce. Jamie was shocked, but he also felt relieved. At least now, he thought, the fighting would stop.

If a couple spends most of their time arguing with each other, they may decide divorce is the best option.

Stress

Stress can also damage or destroy a marriage. If parents are worried about **financial** issues, employment problems, medical problems, or other serious situations, it can be hard for them to focus on the marriage. Stress can lead to arguments and make it hard for people to listen and care about each other as much as they would like. This can lead to divorce.

Sometimes a parent will ask for a divorce because he or she simply isn't happy anymore. A parent might want a different lifestyle and choose to leave the marriage.

Every family is unique. Even if a family has problems, it does not mean that the parents will divorce.

Financial worries can hurt a marriage and lead to divorce.

What do you think?

Some parents stay together even though they are very unhappy and fight a lot. Do you think this is better for their children? Or do you think a divorce would be better for the family?

Changes and Feelings

Since a marriage is a legal arrangement, ending a marriage through divorce involves legal matters too. Depending on where they live and what needs to be done, some couples who divorce need to have solicitors to work out a legal divorce agreement.

The divorce agreement

A divorce agreement involves many issues, such as financial decisions and living arrangements. To work out these issues, the couple often has to go to court, where the divorce is finalized. The entire process of the divorce agreement can take a long time. This time can be stressful for the family.

Divorce is often a complicated and lengthy experience, but it is often a wise decision with long-term benefits for the family.

Some parents hire solicitors to help with the divorce.

Divorce can bring many changes, including moving to a new home.

Many things change after a divorce. One parent usually moves out of the house, or the family might sell the house and everyone moves somewhere else. Everyday **routines** often change too.

Divorce often has financial consequences. A family might have less income than it did before a divorce. Parents may need to move homes, get a different job, or make other changes to make sure the family has enough money. A parent who used to stay home or who only worked part-time may now take a full-time job. Although things can be difficult, most parents try to do what's best for their children and keep the family as stable as possible.

Top tips

It can be difficult to **cope** with the changes that a divorce brings. Here are some tips:

- Understand that both of your parents still love you and want what's best for you.
- Continue to share special times with each parent.
- Always look for something positive in every situation.
- Be patient. Things will get better in time.

How you might feel

It is normal to have different emotions when your parents divorce. Young people often report feeling scared, angry, sad, and guilty.

Scared

It's normal to feel scared and worried about what will happen next. Divorce changes a family forever, and everyone involved worries about what the future will hold. Fear of the future is one of the most common feelings that accompany divorce. Teenagers may want to share their concerns with their parents, who may be feeling scared themselves.

Angry

Anger is another common **reaction** to divorce. Many young people feel angry and betrayed when their parents divorce. They feel angry at their parents for not being able to get along. They're angry at themselves for being stuck in a bad situation. Often, teenagers will take their anger out on their family, friends, and even themselves. They may play up in school, get into fights, or argue with family members and friends.

Most people feel scared and angry when they find out their parents are going to divorce.

Sad

The end of a marriage is a big loss, and it makes most people involved feel very sad. Teenagers wish that their family could go back to the way it was before. They **grieve** over the end of the family being together.

Lonely

Young people caught up in divorce often feel lonely. They miss the parent who no longer lives with them. They may think that no one really understands their feelings or what they're going through. This makes them feel alone.

It can be tough to go about normal activities, such as school, during a divorce.

Top tips

Here are some ways to handle emotions during a divorce:

- Realize that you are not alone.
- Understand that it is okay to feel sad, scared, and angry.
- Find someone to talk to.
- Find positive ways to cope with your feelings. Write about your feelings in a diary or paint a picture of how you feel. Go for a walk when you need time to think.

Guilty

Guilt often strikes young people when they find out their parents are getting a divorce. It is common for teenagers in a divorced family to feel like the divorce was their fault. They imagine that if they had only behaved better, listened better, or done better in school their parents would not have divorced. This is not true. Marriages break up because the parents can no longer get along with each other or no longer want to be married. They don't get divorced because their children did something wrong or because they don't love their children anymore.

Many teenagers feel guilty when their parents divorce, even though the break-up is not their fault.

Some teens imagine that if they can arrange for their parents to spend time together, they will get married again.

Fantasies

Many young people have **fantasies** that their parents will fall in love with each other again. These teenagers might try to find ways to get their parents back together. They might invite both parents to a school event or pretend to be sick so their parents will be drawn back together. However, once parents have decided to divorce, it is very unusual for them to change their minds. A couple getting back together almost never occurs because their children came up with a plan to trick them.

Case study

For two years after her parents divorced, Lisa was obsessed with getting them back together. She tried many different tricks to get her parents to show up at places at the same time. It was only after she spoke to a school **counsellor** that Lisa realized that she could not control what her parents did or how they felt about each other.

Who lives where?

One of the biggest things young people worry about during a divorce is which parent they will live with. Although both parents are expected to take care of their children, the person who has **custody** of a child has most of the responsibility.

Every family makes different custody arrangements. Sometimes one parent will have sole custody. This means that he or she is completely responsible for the child. The child lives with that parent all of the time, but usually visits the other parent.

Many families have joint custody. Each parent is responsible for the child, and the child spends time with each parent. Many parents who divorce want joint custody of their children because it allows both parents to have a say in raising the children.

Many young people split their time between their parents, living with one parent during the week and visiting the other at the weekend.

NEWSFLASH

About 70 percent of children in divorced families live with their mothers. In the past, children in divorced families nearly always lived with their mothers. Today, some children live with their fathers.

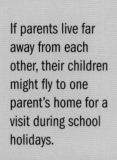
If parents live far away from each other, their children might fly to one parent's home for a visit during school holidays.

Who will I live with?

Young people in divorced families often live with one parent and visit the other parent at the weekend or during holidays. If divorced parents live near each other, their children may alternate homes every few days or every week.

Sometimes, neither parent is able to have custody of their children. If this happens, the children might live with grandparents, other relatives, or family friends. Usually siblings live together, but sometimes one sibling might live with one parent, while another lives with the other parent. Each family needs to find the arrangement that works best for them.

What do you think?

Some courts allow teenagers to have a say in where they will live. The intent is to allow the young person's feelings and desires to be considered, which might make the decision easier on the family. However, other courts feel this arrangement can put too much pressure on young people. Do you think allowing teenagers to have a say is a good idea?

Back and forth

Children and teenagers with divorced parents often spend time living with each parent. This means having two different homes. This arrangement of travelling back and forth can get very confusing. Clothes, homework, sports equipment, and other possessions have to be in the right house at the right time.

There are ways to make living in two different places easier. The key is to be organized. Many families find that it helps to make a calendar of activities for the week. This calendar shows which parent has the children that week, so everyone knows where they are supposed to be. The calendar should also list activities, such as school events, games, rehearsals, and meetings. Each parent should have a schedule of their children's events so everyone gets to the right place at the right time.

It can be a challenge for divorced families to keep track of events and activities.

Getting used to different routines at different homes can be one of the toughest adjustments after a divorce.

Many teens find that it helps to keep special possessions at both homes. Favourite games, toys, books, and music will have to be shared between both households. Some teenagers keep a bag packed with important items, so they can easily carry it from one home to the other.

Who's the boss?

One of the biggest changes to **adjust** to is following different rules at each house. It's normal to find this adjustment very difficult. It is important for young people to remember that they have to follow the rules at each house, even if these rules aren't always the same.

Case study

Ruth spends one week at her mum's house and the next week at her dad's. At first she carried her things back and forth in a suitcase. Now she keeps certain things at her mum's and other things at her dad's and has duplicates of items that she needs at both houses. Ruth sometimes wishes that she could have everything in just one place.

Tug of war

When a teenager is used to living with both parents all of the time, it can be difficult to get used to visiting one parent only on weekends or holidays. Young people in this situation miss the parent they don't live with. They also often feel left out of the other parent's life. They wonder how the other parent is doing.

Social issues

Living in two different houses can also be hard on a young person's social life. A teenager might have to miss a get-together with friends because he or she is at the other parent's house in another town. This parent might not want the teenager to go out with friends when the parent only has a few days to spend with his or her child. This is another area where good communication and **compromise** are important to keep everyone happy.

Some young people feel they have to choose between spending time with the parent they visit and spending time with their friends.

Case study

Whenever Rose and Mark came home from a weekend at their father's, their mother was full of questions about everything they did. Rose and Mark's father was so angry at their mother that he wouldn't talk to her directly. Instead, he sent messages and complaints home through his children. Rose and Mark hated being caught between their parents like this.

Still fighting

Even though a family break-up is painful, it can work out to be a good solution to living in a family that is constantly unhappy. However, if parents didn't get along well before a divorce, there may still be difficulties afterwards. It is common for parents to disagree and fight over issues and for their children to be caught in the middle.

In the middle

Divorced parents sometimes use their children to find out what the other parent is doing. Teenagers don't want to be spies or messengers between their parents. They just want to enjoy their family.

Some parents will **criticize** each other in front of their children. It hurts to hear criticism of one parent or feel like you have to defend one parent to another. The best thing to do is to try to stay out of the middle. Tell your parents you will not take sides. Don't be afraid to speak up about your feelings!

Young people who are caught between parents need to speak up and say how much it hurts to be in the middle.

19

New lives

Life does go on after a divorce. In time, one or both parents may see other people. It can be hard to deal with this. However, it is important to remember that parents want to have friends and companionship just as much as teenagers do.

Getting to know you

Young people should make an effort to get used to the new people in their parents' lives. It is not fair to anyone if a teen automatically acts **hostile** just because he or she is angry that a parent is going out with a new person. Causing trouble in a new **relationship** is not going to get parents back together. It will just make an awkward situation even more unpleasant for everyone.

Of course, it can be hard to get used to a new person in a parent's life. A teenager might feel jealous and compare the new partner to the other parent. It might also be difficult to get on with the new person. These feelings are normal.

It's normal for divorced parents to make new friends and date other people.

The bright side

There can be many positive things about a parent's new relationship. A teenager can make a new friend and have new experiences. He or she may find the new person becomes a good friend or is great to talk to. Most of all, having a new relationship probably makes the parent happier, and that's a good thing too!

When a parent meets someone new, it can be a good thing for the whole family.

Case study

When Julie's dad started dating Sharon, Julie was jealous and angry. She insisted that Sharon wasn't her mum and never could be. When her dad and Sharon got married, Julie insisted that she didn't want another mum. However, as Julie and Sharon got to know each other better, Julie discovered she liked Sharon, and she was able to accept her stepmother.

Becoming part of a stepfamily means accepting new parents and siblings into your life.

Living with a stepfamily

A parent's new partner can sometimes become a teenager's stepmother or stepfather. Suddenly, there is another adult living in the house, making new rules and changing the way things have always been done.

It's normal for a stepparent to make new rules or want things done his or her way. This can be very difficult for teenagers, who might not like someone new telling them what to do. However, if teenagers can give the new rules a try, they may find that they aren't so bad after all. It also helps if the **stepfamily** can work out **guidelines** or rules that everyone can live with.

Many young people find it hard to accept **discipline** from a stepparent. The teenager may claim that the new person is not their "real" father or mother so has no right to make new rules. Each family has to come up with a plan that works best for them. A family meeting can help solve these problems before they start.

Top tips

How can you get on better with a stepparent? Here are some ideas:
- Be fair.
- Remember that you don't have to love your new stepparent straight away.
- Follow the rules, even if they seem unfair.
- Remember that getting used to a new family is just as hard for the stepparent as it is for you.

Brothers and sisters too

Remarriage often brings stepsisters and stepbrothers as well. Getting used to a stepparent can be difficult; getting used to new siblings can be another challenge. New siblings may not get on with each other at first.

It can take time, but often stepsiblings can become very close. Many have shared the experiences of divorce and remarriage, so they may find they have a lot in common and that they share the same feelings. Young people may also enjoy becoming part of a different kind of family.

It's important to recognize that stepsibling relationships are complicated. Some stepsiblings get along very well, while others remain distant. Stepsiblings may spend a lot of time together before their parents marry each other, or they may barely know each other before their families come together. Every situation is unique and has its own challenges and rewards for everyone.

Some stepsiblings become close friends and are a great support to each other.

NEWSFLASH

In the United Kingdom, about 10 percent of families are stepfamilies. Stepfamilies come in all shapes and sizes and form at different times. Young children often welcome a stepparent more easily than older children or teenagers.

Reaching out

You've got a friend

Divorce doesn't just affect the immediate family. It also affects how young people behave with other people in their lives.

Some teenagers find it hard to tell their friends that their parents are getting divorced. They may be embarrassed to admit their family is not perfect, or think that their friends will feel sorry for them or treat them differently.

A close friend who also has divorced parents is a good person to share your feelings with.

The truth is that friends can be a good source of support for young people whose families are facing divorce. This is especially true if the friends' families have gone through a divorce already. Teenagers should not be afraid to talk about their families and share their feelings with close friends who care about them.

Siblings are another great source of support. After all, brothers and sisters share the same experiences and often have some of the same feelings. Talking to siblings and sharing feelings is a great way to feel less alone.

Talk it over

Most of all, teenagers should speak to their parents. Some young people are reluctant to do this. They think that their parents are having enough problems and that it will only make them feel worse if they know their children are hurting too. However, most parents realize that divorce is difficult for their children and want to help them get through it.

Some young people may be so sad, scared, and angry about the divorce that they need to talk to someone besides family members and friends. School counsellors and family **therapists** are specially trained to help people deal with difficult life changes, like divorce. A teenager shouldn't be afraid to seek help at school or ask a parent to find a counsellor he or she can talk to.

A school counsellor can be helpful when dealing with a divorce.

Case study

After his parents divorced, Chris lost interest in friends and activities and spent most of his time lying around watching television. Chris's mum brought him to a counsellor, who helped Chris deal with his feelings. The counsellor encouraged Chris to keep a diary. Over the next few months, Chris started to spend time with his friends again and rejoined the school's football team.

Not your fault

It's common for young people to feel that something they did was the reason for their parents' divorce. Although divorce affects children and teenagers, it is not caused by them. There is nothing they could have done to stop the divorce and nothing they can do to put their family back together. The best thing to do is accept the change and move into the future with confidence.

It's important to remember that even though parents might stop loving each other, they do not stop loving their children. Parents may not always act as nicely as they could, or they may not be around as much as they used to, but they don't stop caring about their family. Even if two people stop being husband and wife, they never stop being parents.

Technology can help members of divorced families stay connected to each other.

After a divorce, a family can still celebrate and have wonderful times together.

It's important for young people to know that it is normal to have painful feelings after a divorce. It's perfectly okay to be sad, scared, or angry. These feelings will not last forever, and things usually get better in time.

Divorce changes many things, but it is not the end of the world. Life does go on, and things will get better. Try to see the divorce as more than the end of a marriage. It can be the start of a new and happier life for the whole family.

NEWSFLASH

It's true that many young people suffer long-lasting effects from living in a divorced family. However, most studies show that children and teenagers are **resilient** and cope very well after a divorce. It is especially helpful if the divorced parents remain friendly to each other and if both parents take an active part in their children's lives.

Facts about divorce

- The United States ranks first in the world when it comes to the divorce rate. It is followed by Puerto Rico, Russia, and the United Kingdom.

- The United Kingdom has the highest divorce rate in Europe.

- More than 20 percent of parents have divorced at least once.

- About 40 percent of first marriages and 70 percent of second marriages now end in divorce.

- First marriages that end in divorce usually last about eight years.

- Most people wait about three years to marry again after a divorce.

- About 700,000 British children live with at least one stepparent.

Glossary

adjust get used to a change

compromise agreement to accept something that is not exactly what you want

cope deal with

counsellor someone who is trained to help people with their problems

criticize complain about someone or something

custody legal right to take care of a child

discipline control over the way someone behaves

fantasy imaginary thoughts and stories that are not likely to happen

financial having to do with money

grieve feel very sad

guidelines rules explaining how something should be done

hostile unfriendly, angry

intend plan

legal having to do with the law

reaction action in response to something

relationship way people get along with each other

resilient able to cope with change

routine usual habits and way of life

separation when a husband and wife stop living together

stepfamily family formed when parents remarry

stress worry, strain, or pressure

therapist someone who is trained to help with emotional problems

Further resources

Divorce is difficult to cope with. If you are dealing with your parents' divorce, remember that you aren't alone. As well as your family and friends, there are many resources available to help you get through your parents' divorce.

Books

Choices and Decisions: When Parents Separate, Pete Sanders and Steve Myers (Franklin Watts, 2006)

Need to Know: Family Break-up, Kelly Bishop and Penny Trip (Heinemann Library, 2003)

Separations: Divorce, Janine Amos (Cherrytree Books, 2007)

Surviving Divorce, Trudi Strain Trueit (Franklin Watts, 2007)

Why Do Families Break Up?, Jane Bingham (Hodder Wayland, 2005)

Websites

Childline
www.childline.org.uk/ContactChildLine.asp
Contact details for Childline are on this page. They can help with whatever problems you may have.

Divorce aid
www.divorceaid.co.uk/child/teenagers.htm
This site talks directly to young people and provides details of other web links and television programmes that give advice on coping with divorce.

Websites (continued)

It's not your fault
www.itsnotyourfault.org/Info_and_advice_for_teenagers.html
This site provides lots of information on helplines and useful websites to help you get through your parents' divorce.

NCH, the children's charity
www.nch.org.uk/contactus/index.php?i=64
This web page provides details of all the contact details for local NCH offices.

Samaritans
www.samaritans.org/talk_to_someone.aspx
The Samaritans are there to help whatever your problem. This web page gives you all the contact details.

Organization

Cafcass National Office
8th Floor
South Quay Plaza 3
189 Marsh Wall
London
E14 9SH
Tel: 020 7510 7000
www.cafcass.gov.uk/
Cafcass is an organization that helps children through the divorce of their parents. The webpage above provides answers to questions about the divorce process for both younger children and teenagers.

Index